Become the next American Ninja Warrior

The Ultimate Guide on how to Prepare and Win the next American Ninja Warrior Obstacle Race

D1396577

Table of Contents

Introduction

In 1997, the Tokyo Broadcasting System began airing *Sasuke*, a series of three-hour, 100-participant obstacle course specials. These self-contained specials were shot in Yokohama, Japan on a studio set dubbed Mount Midoriyama—a sadistic monument built of scaffolding, ropes, and foam pads. Contestants made their way through increasingly difficult stages of unyielding, surrealist obstacles in the hopes of achieving "Total Victory" over Mount Midoriyama.

Olympic athletes, MMA fighters, pro wrestlers, celebrities, entertainers, comedians, and hundreds of normal folks who are badass at climbing up cargo nets have all taken part in *Sasuke*. The U.S. version of the show, now known as *American Ninja Warrior*, has been airing since 2006 and has become a national hit.

To compete on American Ninja Warrior you'll need a certain set of skills. Push around all the weights you want, if you don't train right, you probably won't conquer one obstacle. In order to do well in the competition you'll have to work on your grip, core, and overall endurance when training.

If you think you have what it takes to become the next American Ninja Warrior, then read on.

This book will be your guide, your bible, your new best friend, preparing you to conquer the Ultimate Cliffhanger, Salmon Ladder, and other obstacles becoming the next Joe Moravsky or Kacy Catanzaro.

Thanks again for purchasing this book, I hope you will enjoy it!

Chapter 1: The American Ninja Warrior Competition

The American Ninja Warrior obstacle course competition is a television series that has been airing on NBC since 2009. The competition was created as a spin-off of *Sasuke,* literally meaning "Excellence" held in Japan since 1997. Sasuke has gradually become a worldwide sensation as 100 competitors, including fishermen, postal workers, teachers, doctors and carpenters, who train year-round, put their jobs on hold to fight for total victory, or "kanzenseiha" at Mount Midoriyama. Of over 2,900 attempts only 3 people have achieved kanzenseiha (One person won it twice). Every time someone is crowned champion, the obstacle course is completely redesigned.

Since the inception of the show, seven spin-offs in different countries were created, including NBC's "American Ninja Warrior" (NBC owns G4, the channel that airs *Sasuke).* In order to win the grand prize of $500,000, competitors face four tough stages, each one harder than the previous one. The tournament culminates at the last stage, Mount Midoriyama staged in Las Vegas, which consists of a challenging rope climb. Ultimately, all winners of the American Ninja Warrior will then compete in *Sasuke,* against Japanese competitors.

Originally, the American Ninja Warrior Competition was held in Japan's Mount Midoriyama after a series of qualifying rounds in Los Angeles; but since 2012, the competition venue has changed to Las Vegas, Nevada, with a makeshift Mount Midoriyama, as the producers thought that bringing all the competitors to Japan each and every year would just be too taxing, literally and figuratively.

The Stages of the Competition

The tournament consists of four stages with increasing difficulty. The obstacles are built on metal structures with water below to

4

soften the impact should a competitor fall. In order to pass a stage and advance to the next, all obstacles have to be mastered without falling. This may sound easier than it is. Anyone who has watched the famous TV series will understand that not only pure strength, but also flexibility, endurance and mental stamina are required to make it through a stage.

Stage 1. In this stage competitors compete against each other for the 30 fastest times in order to advance to stage 2. While in Japan only 100 competitors can run the course, American Ninja Warrior has not set a limit on how many people can compete in this stage. Some obstacles change every season, but some of the constant obstacles in stage 1 are the "Jumping Spider", "Half Pipe Attack" and "Warped Wall". Major core strength is required for all stages, but stage 1 also requires you to have balance and flexibility.

Stage 2. In this stage, the competitors not only have to compete against one another, they also have to compete with the race itself by going through harder obstacles than the first stage. The 15 best competitors will advance to the next round. Some notable obstacles in this stage are the "Double Salmon Ladder", "Unstable Bridge", "Balance Tank", the "Metal Spin" and the "Wall Lift". Again, aside from the all-important core strength, great focus should be given to balance and leg strength.

Stage 3. This is the stage where most athletes fail and consequently return to their homes, training hard for the next season. Stage three requires huge upper body strength and of course core strength. Some crazy obstacles include "Pipe Jungle", "Ultimate Cliffhanger", "Doorknob Grasper", "Floating Boards", the "Spider Flip" and the sadistic "Flying Bar".

Before we go into the best preparation techniques let's focus first on how to apply to American Ninja Warrior.

Chapter 2: The Application Process

Applications for each season of the American Ninja Warrior Competition happen at least 2 months before the tryouts, which are held in:

- Pittsburgh, Pennsylvania

- Orlando, Florida

- Kansas City, Missouri

- Venice Beach, California

Go to http://www.adeignco.com/AmericanNinjaWarrior/ to apply to compete on the show. On this website you will also get dates for submission deadlines, the regional qualifiers and the final.

If you live far away from the above listed venues, you may still fill out an application form found on the above website. You'll then be told by the producers at which venue to audition, most likely the one that's nearest you, or wherever they see fit. There will be two stages of regional qualifying rounds, which are "qualifiers", and "finals". Winners of the regional finals will then compete in Las Vegas, Nevada, to see who will compete in Mount Miyodori in Japan for *Sasuke*.

Requirements

- If you want to try out, make sure that you are:

- At least 21 years of age;

- Living in the United States, and is a legal resident of the country;

- Free during the scheduled times and dates for auditions;

- Sure that your health is in tip-top shape and that you can join in challenging and exhausting activities, and;

- Willing to submit a 2 to 3 minute video introducing yourself together with your clear digital photo and application details to http://www.anwcasting.com/, so you could qualify.

Fill out the online application form completely with no typos. Have your friend read it over before hitting the submit button. You submission video is extremely important. Read the below tips carefully:

Make an inspirational video. Sell yourself to the camera and to the producers. You'll be on TV! Naturally, the producers are looking for both, great personalities and great athletes. Talking about an inspirational life event, having an interesting side hobby, showing off with your odd career as commercial diver, or salmon fisherman, or any other interesting story about your life will be a huge component in getting you picked for the show. You'll be picked by TV producers, which means that great personalities will oftentimes win over solid athletes.

Be energetic. Show your passion about your training routine, your hometown, your personal life, your wife or girlfriend, etc. Filming every aspect of you and your training and demonstrating hometown pride has been a huge factor in being a stand-out submission video.

Create a high quality video. Don't submit a video that you took from your new iPhone 6. I don't mean to belittle the new iPhone, but having good lighting, a tripod to ensure steady filming, crisp audio, and maybe some creative editing will go a long way.

Now that you have submitted your online application, along with your high quality, inspirational video, let's focus on the work out routines and proper nutrition that will get you through all four stages.

Note: Even though you may not be selected to go on the show, you will still have the chance to "walk on" on the day of the regional qualifiers. Prepare to arrive at least one week ahead of time and bring a friend and a tent. You'll have to make sure you reserve your spot among the first ten people in line.

Chapter 3: The American Ninja Workout

I am assuming, if you are reading this you are committed to putting in hard work and effort in order to get in fighting fit form. There are no shortcuts to successfully completing a stage, much less wining the champion's title. Before you rush to the gym and start pushing iron, you should first make an overall training plan. Rather than focusing on building overall muscle, start focusing on specific areas, such as:

- Overall core strength

- Grip strength

- Brachiate, monkey swing from branch to branch

- Explosive upper body strength

- Obstacle training

- Footwork

- Balance

If you have followed the previous seasons of American Ninja Warrior, you may have noticed that two types of athletes do extremely well – rock climbers and parkour practitioners.

Your first order of business is to sign up for a rock climbing gym with boulder area or a parkour gym. It will be ideal if the gym has a weight room. Otherwise, sign up for a weight gym.

Plan on exercising at least five, preferably six times a day. Alternating one week with five work out days and the other with six will work, too. It is important to have your rest days and not get "over-trained", which will lead to injuries, such as stress fractures and muscle tears. Injuries are much less likely to occur when you are not over-taxing your body, and avoiding injuries is of utmost importance to avoiding setbacks in your training.

Ideally, you will have access to obstacles, either at your parkour gym or self-made ones in your back yard. You can buy cheap blueprints for American Ninja Warrior obstacles online and build the most challenging ones, such as the Salmon Ladder, Cliffhanger and Jumping Spider. This way you can train the movements involved with each obstacle. We'll analyze each obstacle a little later.

Eat good! This doesn't mean eating five hamburgers and a McDonald salad. Believe it or not, but having the right diet regiment is just as important as being physically strong.

Next, you'll see a sample work out plan that will ensure you will be well prepared for each obstacle you will face. Remember to set yourself small goals. Adding one more pull up, or climbing one grade harder etc. will ensure you stay motivated throughout your training period.

Please note that you should be healthy. If there is a doubt, please first see your doctor to get approved for the rigorous work out regiment that follows. I am also assuming you are fairly fit and have seen a gym from the inside before. If some exercises seem impossible or you can't finish the recommended number of repetitions and sets, don't worry. Do as many as you can. By repeatedly doing these workouts and staying motivated you will quickly get stronger and fitter. Before each workout warm-up by on a cycle or treadmill and stretch your muscles for at least 15 minutes (shoulders, forearms, chest, back, legs, etc).

Please also note that, if you are new to rock-climbing, you should calculate at least three more months of preparation time, as you will have to build up basic strength and technique before continuing with the below intermediate to advanced workouts. Once you sign up for a rock climbing membership, enroll into a couple of climbing classes and start working your way up on the boulder problems. Bouldering will ensure you build core strength on the overhangs and grip strength on the various types of holds.

The Schedule

<u>Monday</u>

AM: Go for an early 5 to 8 mile run.

> If you live near a forest or other non-paved trails, I highly recommend you run cross-country style, jumping over tree stump, avoiding rocks and snakes, dodging branches and running downhill trying not to slide. This will not only increase your endurance, but also greatly improve your footwork.

> Use a heart rate monitor to stay between 70% and 80% of your training zone (to be determined by you with below instructions), which will avoid you depleting your body's glycogen stores, ensuring that you will have the energy to perform an intense afternoon workout. In order to calculate the optimal heart rate for your runs, you need to first determine the various work-rate zones for your heart, and use these zones to guide your work-rate during your runs. The first thing you will need to do in order to accomplish this is to figure out two key values.

> Your maximum heart rate (MHR), which is the fastest rate your heart is able to beat per minute. To get a quick estimate this rate, subtract half of your age from the number 205. To perform an actual test on yourself, do interval training, preferably on a hill of at least 200 or 300 yards or meters in length. Sprint up the hill and jog back down. Without resting, repeat this cycle for five or six times, and you will likely attain a heart rate that is at least very near your MHR. In the absence of a hill, you may wish to extend the length of your intervals to 400 meters.

> Your resting heart rate (RHR), the rate at which your heart beats when you are completely at rest and in the absence of stressful external stimuli, like caffeine, loud music, or an onsetting illness. Unlike your MHR, which is essentially fixed, the RHR is an indicator of your overall level of fitness, and

slowly decreases in people who are more fit. Generally, the RHR of each individuals can vary greatly. People leading an inactive lifestyle may have a RHR close to or even beyond 100 beats per minute. Most endurance athletes will have a RHR below 60 or 50 beats per minute, and sometimes even below 40 beats per minute. The absolute lowest RHRs belong to elite runners, some of which dip below 30 beats per minute. The reason for the low heart beat in fit people is that the stroke volume is so high that each heartbeat pumps sometimes more than twice as much blood as that of a inactive adult. This causes the heart rate to slow down substantially, while still supplying the entire body with adequate blood flow, and thus oxygen. A heart with a large stroke volume means that it is a strong heart, resulting from a high level of aerobic fitness.

The best way to determine your RHR is to strap on your heart rate monitor, first thing in the morning, even before getting out of bed. Just lying in your bed for two to three minutes will give you a pretty accurate estimate of your RHR.

Now you are ready to calculate your training zones and set up your customized chart, indicating how much strain you are putting on your heart at a given rate. With the below formula, create a chart with 5% increments, all the way up to 100%, your MHR.

((MHR-RHR) x Percent Level) + RHR

For example: assume your MHR is 180 and your RHR is 85, your calculation for a 95% level would be:

((180-85) x 95%) + 85 = 175 beats per minute

Perform this calculation for 90%, 85%, 80%, all the way to 5% and RHR. Note the results on your chart, which will be extremely helpful with your training program.

PM: In the afternoon, head to your local rock climbing gym, and do following work-outs.

1. **Warm up** on an easy boulder problem, climbing up and down five times.

2. Do 100 **Crunches** and 4 sets of 10 **Jack Knives**

3. For the crunches, lie down on your back, set your feet shoulder-wide apart, keep your back flat on the ground and as you come up, exhale slowly, focusing on the tension in your abs.

4. For the Jack Knives, lie down flat on your back, extend your arms backwards and bring your arms and extended legs up simultaneously. Try touching your ankles with your extended arms and always keep a controlled, good form.

5. Head to the **hang-board** (If you can spend around $80, get the Metolius Simulator 3D Training Board or the Metolius Rock Rings, which will give you an insane boost in grip strength and finger strength) and do:

   - 5-10 Five second deadhangs on

   - Crimps

   - Pinches

   - Slopers

   - Pockets

6. Now you are warmed up for the **100 pull-up workout**.

   - 8 Frenchies, with each Frenchie consisting of

   - One full pull-up, lock off for 5 seconds and go down

   - Without resting, or touching the ground, do another pull-up all the way up and lock off with your arms at 45 degrees.

- Without resting, or touching the ground, do another pull-up all the way up and lock off with your arms at 90 degrees.

- Without resting, or touching the ground, do another pull-up all the way up and lock off with your arms at 120 degrees.

- 8 times 6 uneven pull-ups. Four on each side.

- With one hand at least 5 inches higher than the other one, do 6 pull-ups.

- Repeat with the other hand higher

- 20 regular pull-ups

- Lock off for a couple of seconds before slowly lowering your body

7. Finish with a **campus workout.** Extreme caution is required when starting this workout routine, as you may injure your tendons. This is an advanced workout and should only be done once you have built up solid finger strength.

   - Ladder. Climb the campus board like a ladder, alternating hands for each rung going up and down.

   - Bumps. Bump one hand up two rungs and back down, then bump the other hand up.

   - Lock-Offs. Bump one hand up until you can't go any higher and come back down. Then bump the other hand up.

   - Double Clutches. Here you bump both hands up one rung simultaneously, going up and down the campus board.

Campus training, while extremely hard on your tendons, will ensure you build insane finger strength and conquer the Cliffhanger obstacle with ease.

8. Hanging **rock balls**, same as the Cannonball Alley obstacle. If your gym has these little devils, you should definitely take advantage of them. These are grapefruit sized balls suspended on two straps.

    - Grab both rock balls and while locking off one arm, extend the other one all the way out, repeating this 10 times for each arm.

    - Lock off one arm, while quickly letting go with the other hand. Switch hands and repeat 10 times

    - Finish off with one Frenchie

9. If are still not tired at this point, round off the day with a fun **bouldering session** with your friends.

Tuesday

This will be a climbing focused day. Head to your rock climbing gym, warm up on a cycle or treadmill, stretch your muscles, especially your fingers and forearms and do a few pull-ups.

I personally like to warm up my fingers, climbing up some walls on an "Autobelay" system, but you may also do an easy traverse or easy boulder problems. The main point here is that you choose a warm up climb with big holds.

Increase the difficulty of your boulder problems until you reach your limit. Work on a few problems to learn new moves, refine your hand-foot co-ordination and have fun. Keep bouldering until your forearms and fingers scream.

Start traversing boulder and climbing walls until you literally falls off. Try to build up your endurance to at least half an hour of traversing.

Do 100 push-ups. You may vary those by using push up handles, resting your feet on a workout bench or in TRX bands.

Finish off with as many Frenchies as you can do.

<u>Wednesday</u>

AM: Go for an early 5 to 8 mile run

PM: Head to the gym, warm up and stretch.

1. **Warm up** on an easy boulder problem, climbing up and down 5 times

2. Get ready for **4x4s,** which consists of climbing four sets of four boulder problems back-to-back. Each set is separated by a 4 minute rest period. This workout will build you anaerobic endurance, which is all so critical in Stage 3 of the American ninja competition. You'll keep doing this routine once a week all the way until your competition day.

   First of all, this is an intensive work-out and it will have you breathing hard. Be sure to push through your pain and give your ultimate.

   - Pick four boulder problems that are at your "onsight" limit, meaning a grade that you can usually climb on first attempt, but not too easy.

   - Repeat the first problem four times in a row, without resting.

   - Rest for 4 minutes and continue to the next problem, climbing it four times in a row.

   - Complete all four boulder problems, which should take you around 25-30 minutes.

   You can take notes of how many times you fell, how crappy you felt, or what grades you climbed.

Stick with it. Go all the way with this. The place you'll see the biggest improvement is when you're feeling "flat" toward the end of a cycle. If you can push through this time, you're in there. Keep your mind looking forward, and forget about feeling "fit" or "in shape," we're looking to surpass that level.

3. At this point you should feel pretty exhausted and we're almost done. Just a couple more **leg workouts**. The Bulgarian Split Squat, Single Leg Deadlift, and the One-Legged Squat

   - For the Bulgarian Split Squat grab two 20 lbs dumbbells and a knee-high stool, which should be located behind you. Reach one leg back and rest one the stool, hold the dumbbells in your hands and squat down, ensuring your knee does not go over the shin and your back knee almost touches the ground. Do 3 sets of 8-12 reps for each knee.

   - The Single Leg Deadlift works stability and balance. Again hold two 20-30 lbs dumbbells in your hands, stand on one leg and lower the dumbbells on the side of your body bending the knee slightly, pushing hips back and balancing with your other leg. Keep your weight on your heel. Do 4 sets for each leg.

   - The Single Leg Squat has you standing on one leg and squatting down, while balancing with your other leg to the front. Make sure to keep your weight on the heel and your shins in a vertical line.

4. If you still have some gas in the tank you can finish your training off bouldering with you buddies, trying to solve some hard bouldering problems.

Thursday

This will be your off day. Recover from the hard days of training. Eat plenty of food, drink lots of water and get some rest. Go to bed early and get ready for the next day.

Friday

This is a repeat of Monday's workout. To mix things up, instead of running, you may choose to go practice Parkour, or go mountain biking or swimming. It is important to switch up your routines, so that you don't tire mentally and stay focused on your ultimate goal. Repeat the Hang-Board exercises, 100 Pull-Up Workout, Campus Board, and Rock Balls.

Saturday

1. Climb. Climb. Climb. Focus on general climbing technique and tackling tougher problems. Climb for an intense one hour session and then head to the weight room.

2. Work on your core and abs Choose 3 of the following exercises and do 4 sets for each: Abs Wheel, Arms high partial sit-up, Dip/Leg-Raise Combo, Plank, Side Plank, Medicine Ball Russian Twist, Hanging Legg Raises. TRX Snaps, Jack Knives.

   - Abs Wheel. One of my favorites. This exercise will rock your core. Kneel on your knees and roll forward on the Abs Wheel. If you are really strong you can raise your legs off, with your toes being the only other contact to the ground. Do 15 reps, increasing to 20 reps

   - Arms high partial sit-up. Similar to the crunch, lie on your back, feet flat on the ground, knees shoulder wide apart and raise your arms up. Now lift your upper body, similar to the crunch.

- Dip/Leg Raises Combo. Get on a dip bar, bend down doing one dip with your legs raised forward. As you come up, circle your outstretched legs in front of you two times clockwise, and two times counter clockwise. Go back down into the dip. Repeat 5 times, working your way up to 10 times.

- Plank. A climber's essential. Go into Plank position resting your weight on your forearms and toes, shoulder wide apart. Stay in plank position with a straight back at least one minute, working your way up to 3 minutes. You may also put a medicine ball on your hips and the roll it off as you start struggling.

- Side Plank. Another climber's essential for major core. Lie down on your side, resting you weight on your forearms, or hand, lift the other arm straight up. Keep your body in one straight line and stop your hips from sagging down. One minute to start, working your way up to two minutes for each side.

- Medicine Ball Russian Twist. Sit down, with your legs bent and feet flat on the ground. Hold a 20lbs medicine in your hands and rotate your upper body from side to side. Do 20 reps.

- Hanging Leg Raises. Hang from a pull-up bar and raise your outstretched legs up in front of you. Do 20 reps.

- TRX Snaps. Your feet will be in two TRX straps, a few inches above the ground. Stretch out your body and rest on your forearms. Now you snap your body, bringing your knees to your chest. Do 20 quick repetitions.

- Jack Knives. As described earlier, lie down flat on your back, extend your arms backwards and bring your arms and extended legs up simultaneously. Try touching your ankles with your extended arms and always keep a controlled, good form.

Sunday

Sunday is a "fun day". This should be a "wildcard" day, depending on how you feel. If you feel your body needs rest, then follow your body's request. If you feel like having fun, playing on some outside boulder problems, running on the beach, or playing on your home-made American Ninja Obstacles in your backyard then go with it. If you have enough energy for a workout, head to the gym and do a "non-traditional" workout, meaning you work on muscle groups you don't focus on too much, such as chest (doing push-ups, Dumbbell Bench Press, Cable Flies, Incline, Decline), shoulder (shoulder pushups, handstand pushup against wall, dumbbell front raise and side raise), or Legs (military press, deadlifts, squats in varying foot and leg positions).

You should do pull-ups on a daily basis. Whenever you see a bar, you should jump on it and do a few reps. As mentioned before, I highly recommend you purchase a hang-board, which can be installed above your door frame. You'll then be able to practice regular pull-ups in varying hand positions and strengthen you fingers and core. The hang board usually comes with some great workouts suggestions. Be sure to always warm up to avoid tendon injuries. Lastly, if you have an option to train on the actual American Ninja Obstacles, train on them whenever possible to get you comfortable with how they behave.

Chapter 4 Conquering tough Obstacles

Salmon Ladder

The Salmon Ladder is by far the most dreaded obstacle on Sasuke and American Ninja Warrior, taking out competitors by the dozen. The Salmon Ladder evolved from a one-sided ladder to a double-sided ladder, and now most recently a swap salmon ladder, which is essentially a series of double salmon ladder, forcing competitors to switch directions several times. To get past this obstacles, you'll need more than raw physical strength. Unlike the Ultimate Cliffhanger or the Unstable Bridge, the Salmon Ladder is highly technical and brings a high level of respect, due to so many apparently strong people failing on it. To get past the mental fear and acquire proper technique, I recommend you build a salmon ladder, which can easily and quickly be done:

- Get two sturdy beams (or four for a double salmon ladder) and secure them into the ground around four feet apart. If you can find two trees spaced around four feet from each other, you can also use them.

- Purchase heavy duty, thick nails at Home Depot and hammer them into the beams/trees at a 35 degree angle and have them sticking out approximately three inches.

- Repeat the above steps going up the beams/trees, spacing the rungs 12 inches apart until you reach 12 feet in height.

- Lastly buy a sturdy, wooden bar, or aluminum bar that will hold your weight when hanging from it.

Start training and eliminate your mental respect for this obstacle.

Unstable Bridge

The Unstable Bridge, while looking like a harmless obstacle that can easily be conquered with solid upper body strength keeps eliminating competitor after competitor, including Youuji Urushihara (Grand Champion) and Drew Dreschel (3 time American Ninja Warrior finalist). To tackle this obstacle you need to develop a combination of upper body strength, grip strength, and core strength to finish the gap jump. What makes this obstacle so tough is that it comes up pretty late into the stage. By the time you reach the Unstable Bridge, your arms are pumping from the salmon ladder. The key skill, aside from the obvious upper arm strength is momentum. If you are a bit creative you can build your own Unstable Bridge, hanging from a 9 foot support beam.

- You can build two bridges with 2x4s or sturdy plywood and secure them to the support beam. Drill four holes on each corner and thread four ropes through the first bridge, securing them with a knot on the other side.

- On the second bridge thread two ropes through the holes on each center end and again securing them with a knot on the other side of the hole

Following are the dimensions:

- Bridge length is 4 feet

- Bridge Width is 1.5 feet

- Bridge Thickness is 1.25 inches

- Gap between two bridges is 1 foot

- Support beam should be at least 9 feet long

The most important tip to conquer this obstacle is to keep your arms at a 90 degree angle. Do not let your arms hang or go straight as this will make it a lot harder to control your shuffling along the bridge.

Jumping Spider

The Jumping Spider has is a tricky obstacle and eliminates the best competitors. Again, same as with the Salmon Ladder, you have to get over your mental block first and realize that this obstacle on its on is not that hard. Rather than strength, you need a whole lot of momentum and mental focus. Aim forward AND high at approximately a 45 to 55 degree angle. As soon as you make contact push your arms and legs out and stop your forward momentum. You can practice the sudden pushing movement between door frames. If you have a Parkour running gym close to you, I do recommend changing up your workouts with occasional Parkour obstacle running and training. Not only will this give you confidence and eliminate your "fear" of mental and physical obstacles, but also improve body control, building strength, endurance, flexibility, balance, agility and explosive strength. If you don't have a Parkour gym in your area, just go outside and use natural or manmade obstacles for your training sessions. Even though you may think your area doesn't feature enough obstacles, the whole spirit of Parkour is to use whatever obstacles come your way. Even a simple rail or a wall may be great training tools.

Cliffhanger

The most dreaded obstacle on American Ninja Warrior. This obstacle is all upper body and finger strength. If you are doing your workouts, especially campus training you should conquer this obstacle in a breeze. What makes it so hard is that by the time you reach this obstacle you are insanely pumped from the previous obstacles. Build up your endurance in the rock climbing gym by doing your 4x4 drills and traverses. Build up to at least half an hour of traversing without touching the ground.

A note on overcoming obstacles by practicing Parkour

Parkour, or sometimes also called Freerunning, has become quite popular over the past few years. Parkour teaches your body and mind to overcome various obstacles with speed and efficiency, requiring the need for adaptability, creativity, and strategy. In order to successfully overcome an obstacle (and not get hurt!) parkour athletes, also known as traceurs and traceuses learn to see the environment in a different way, using movements such as vaulting, running, climbing, swinging, and balancing to pass over, under, and through obstacles. If you have a Parkour running gym close to you, I do recommend changing up your workouts with occasional Parkour obstacle running and training. Not only will this give you confidence and teach you to face fear, set goals, and think critically in order to overcome mental and physical obstacles, but also improve body control and build strength, endurance, flexibility, balance, agility and explosive strength. If you don't have a Parkour gym in your area, just go outside and use natural or manmade obstacles for your training sessions. Even though you may think your area doesn't feature enough obstacles, the whole spirit of Parkour is to use whatever obstacles come your way. Even a simple rail or a wall may be great training tools.

Chapter 5: Ninja Nutrition

To effectively prepare for the American Ninja Warrior competition you need to ensure that your body is in excellent condition. Training without the right fuel will not get you very far. As mentioned before, I recommend you start your training at least one year before the try-outs. During that time you will be have to train hard and often, requiring you to approach each work out with energy and vigor. Remember "You are what you eat!" First and foremost, cut out all processed foods, including your favorite McDonalds cheeseburger, soda, and French fries. I generally recommend you prepare your own meals, so you know what ingredients have been used. Most restaurants use too much unhealthy Canola Oil, which you would want to replace with Coconut or Avocado Oil. It is essential that you maintain a balanced diet, consisting of protein, carbs and fiber.

The Paleo Diet

The Paleo diet is the perfect diet for competitive athletes because it is the only nutritional approach that works with your genetics to help you stay lean, strong and energetic. Recent research in biology, biochemistry, ophthalmology and many other disciplines has shown that a diet consisting of refined foods, trans-fats and sugar is the main culprit for degenerative diseases such as obesity, cancer, diabetes, heart disease, and countless more diseases – not to mention low energy and lack of performance as a consequence.

In a nutshell, the Paleo diet consists of fibrous foods, such as fruits and vegetables, replenishing your body with anti-oxidants, minerals and enzymes, and protein foods ensuring healthy muscle condition and overall energy. Without going too much into diet specifics, I will provide you with a weekly meal plan. Follow this plan for two weeks and feel the difference in your energy levels, your overall well-being, as well as your body leanness.

Here is a simple overview of the Paleo Diet "eat" and "don't eat" list.

EAT

Grass-fed meats. Eat all types of meats, avoiding highly fatty cuts. I recommend poultry, turkey, pork, beef, bison, goose, and duck.

Fish/seafood. Seafood is usually very lean. Try eating bass, salmon, red snapper, trout, halibut, tuna, crab, shrimp, and lobster.

Fresh fruits. Fruits that are low in sugar can be helpful because they can boost your energy and make you feel refreshed and rejuvenated. These fruits are lime, lemon, orange, apple, pear, pumpkin, squash, zucchini, tomato, cucumber, bell pepper, and avocado.

Fresh vegetables. Recommended vegetables are water chestnuts, parsley, jicama, scallions, shallots, fennel, leek, garlic, asparagus, turnip, watercress, radishes, bok choy, celery, green beans, alfalfa sprouts, artichokes, sauerkraut, Brussels sprouts, cauliflower, mushrooms, onions, cabbage, chard, kale, broccoli, spinach, collard, and other greens.

Starchy vegetables. I like adding these to my diet to give me a certain fullness feeling without feeling sluggish. Eat butternut squash, yams, sweet potato and beets.

Eggs. I love eggs. They contain the best protein and taste great. Try different kinds, such as chicken, duck, quail, and ostrich.

Nuts. These are great snacks for in between work-outs. Eat plenty of almonds, cashews, hazelnuts, brazil nuts, walnuts, and pecans.

Seeds. Seeds can be added to all kinds of dishes, giving you and added energy boost. Some seeds I highly recommend are sunflower seeds, pumpkin seeds, chia seeds and flax seeds.

Healthy oils. Your body needs fat – the good kind of fat. Healthy fats are essential to help turn glucose to fuel for your body to be active and alive Cook with coconut oil and avocado, use olive oil, walnut oil and pumpkin seed oil on your salads (remember not to heat olive oil), and add fish oil to your favorite curries.

Condiments, Seasonings, and Herbs. Hot sauce, salsa, tapenade, horseradish, and mustard are your best picks. Avoid packaged ones as much as you can. Check if something contains a lot of sugar or soy. Go for less sodium products instead.

DON'T EAT

Fatty meats such as hot dogs, spam, or other low quality cuts

Cereal grains

Legumes including beans, peas, lentils, soybeans, tofu, peanuts, peanut butter, miso, etc.)

Dairy

Refined sugar and artificial sweeteners

Potatoes

Processed foods

Overly salty foods

Refined vegetable oils

Candy/junk/processed food

Fruit Juices

Alcohol

Sodas

Sample Meal Plans

I am including a few sample meal plans, giving you quick and easy options for making delicious meals that fuel your body to be in competing shape all day, every day. Feel free to mix it up and make variations as you like with the above "eat/don't eat" guide as your reference. Obviously, there are hundreds of tasty recipes for the Paleo diet. The below recipes, which I have personally tested and tried, are merely a starting point for you. For me, it is important to have a tasty meal without standing in the kitchen for too long. I also like to make big portions, giving me great left over meals the next day.

Breakfast

California Omelet

- 4-5 cage-free eggs

- 1 tsp avocado oil

- 1 Onion, chopped

- 1 cup spinach, chopped

- 1 tsp fresh basil

- 1 handful cocktail tomatoes, cut into halves

- 1 Avocado, cut into slices

- 2 strips of bacon (optional)

- Salt and Pepper

Break the eggs into a bowl, add salt and pepper and whisk until well mixed. Heat pan and brown onions until glassy. Add egg mixture and fry for a minute. Then add spinach, tomatoes and basil and spread over egg mixture. Now flip one side over the other and cook until egg mixture is not liquid anymore. Serve with Avocados on the side and with your favorite hot sauce.

Power Shake

- 1 small red beet, or cut a big one in half

- 1 carrot

- 2 leaves of kale

- 1 Celery

- 1 thumb Ginger

- 1 Orange

- 1 Apple

- 1 Banana

- 1tsp Avocado Oil or Coconut Oil

Peel and cut ingredients into a blender, add 2 to 3 cups of drinking water and oil and blend for a minute until all ingredients are pureed. Serving amount ca. 4 cups. Consume right away.

Note: This recipe ensures you will be fueled up with vitamins and minerals for the day ahead. I recommend that you use organic fruits and vegetables. For more information in different kinds of juices, refer to the Appendix with my book referrals.

Carrot and Zucchini Scramble

- 4-5 cage-free eggs

- 1 Carrot, chopped, preferably in food processor

- 1 Zucchini, chopped, preferably in food processor

- 1 tsp Coconut Oil

- Salt and Pepper

Heat oil in pan, add carrot and zucchini and fry for a minute, stirring frequently. Add eggs, salt and pepper to taste and stir frequently until eggs are solid.

Coconut Flour Pancakes

- 3 tbsp Coconut Flour

- 3 Eggs

- 2 tbsp unsweetened apple sauce

- 3-4 tbsp Coconut Milk

- 1 tsp Coconut Oil

- ¼ tsp Baking Soda

- 1-2 tbsp Coconut Sugar

- ¼ tsp Organic Apple Cider Vinegar

Mix flour and eggs until you have a smooth paste. Add apple sauce, coconut milk and coconut sugar, stirring until smooth. Right before cooking, add vinegar and baking soda. Heat oil in pan and add small portions of pancake mixture, browning on both sides. Eat with fresh fruit and raw honey or with strawberry sauce (1 cup strawberries, 2 tbsp coconut cream and 1 tbsp honey, blended).

Lunch

Ceviche

- 1 lbs fresh fish fillet

- 5 limes

- 4 cloves garlic

- 1 tbsp fresh cilantro

- 1 jalapeno chili

- 1 small red onion, sliced

- 8 large romaine lettuce leaves

- 1 Avocado, diced

- 1 tomato diced

- Salt and Pepper

- Hot Sauce

Cube fish and place into glass bowl. Juice limes into food processor, add garlic, cilantro, and seeded jalapeno. Mince into fine pieces. Combine with fish and add onion. Marinate it overnight. Before eating remove most lime juice, leaving fish moist and add salt and pepper. You can double the recipe to have lunch for two days. The lime acts as a natural preservative for the fish.

Chicken Salad

- 1 lbs organic chicken

- ½ cup diced red bell pepper

- 1 artichoke heart, cooked and chopped

- 2 scallions, thinly sliced\

- 1 tbsp fresh parsley, minced

- 1/3 cup Mayonnaise (optional: mixed with 1 tbsp lemon and one garlic clove)

- 1 tsp Coconut Oil

- 1 Avocado

Heat oil in pan and add chicken. Lightly season with salt and pepper. When chicken is well cooked remove from heat and combine with other ingredients in a bowl. Mix well and serve with a fresh Avocado on the side.

Oven roasted vegetable

- 1 Zucchini, cut in small pieces

- 1 yellow Squash

- 1 red, 1 yellow bell pepper de-seeded and cut into small pieces

- 1 lbs green asparagus cut into small pieces

- 1 red onion

- Salt and Pepper

- 2 tsp Coconut Oil

Heat oven to 450F. Combine all veggies into a roasting pan. Add oil, salt and pepper and mix well. Spread veggies out. Roast for 30 minutes until golden brown. You can keep the left overs in the fridge and eat cold at a later time.

Dinner

Chicken Curry

- 6 boneless chicken thighs (organic if possible)

- 1 onion, chopped

- 1 cup coconut milk or pumpkin puree (using canned puree is fine)

- 2 medium zucchinis, sliced

- 2 cups crimini mushrooms

- ½ tsp Turmeric powder

- ½ tsp Paprika powder

- 1 tsp red pepper flakes

- 1 tsp Cumin

- 2 tbsp Coconut Oil

Heat oil in pan and add onions until browned. Add spices to onions and keep stirring for a minute or two until well fragrant. Add chicken and cook until sides turn white. Now add coconut milk or pumpkin puree with a little bit of water, stirring well. Cover and let the curry simmer and acquire flavor. After 10 minutes add zucchinis and mushrooms. Let it cook for 5 more minutes and serve with fresh cilantro and a dash of coconut cream.

I personally make a huge portion, which I can warm up the next two days. Remember curries get better as they sit in your fridge.

Steak and Sweet Potatoes

- 1 steak cut of your choice (Sirloin or New York are my favorites)

- Salt and pepper

- 2 tsp Avocado Oil

- 1 lbs sweet potatoes

Peel sweet potatoes and cut in half. Make sure the potato pieces are not too big. Heat your oven to 350F and bake potatoes for at least on hour. You'll know they are done, when they are nice and soft and taste sweet. In the meantime, season steak with salt and pepper and sprinkle with some avocado oil. 10 minutes before the potatoes are done, heat the oil in an iron skillet and add your steak, frying it to your liking. I prefer medium-rare, so I leave the steak for a one to two minutes on each side. Add one sliced onion to the skillet, if you like some extra flavor. Eating an avocado on the side will taste great.

Beef Chili

- 2 lbs ground beef

- 1 red green bell pepper

- 1 large onion, diced

- 5 medium garlic cloves

- 2 tbsp Avocado Oil

- 2 fresh tomatoes, diced

- 1 Jalapeno, de-seeded and cut in small pieces

- 3 tbsp Cumin powder

- 2 tbsp Chili powder

Heat oil in pan and add onion. Add ground beef and season with salt and pepper. When beef is almost fully cooked through add Cumin and Chili powders, stirring well. Add all the rest of the ingredients and add drinking water to cover all the ingredients. Let chili simmer for an hour, stirring occasionally.

Snacks

- **Nuts**. You can get a whole bag of unsalted, mixed nuts at Sprouts and mix them with raisins or craisins.

- **Banana Bread**. I make Paleo banana bread once a week and eat it whenever I have food cravings.

- **Avocadoes.** You can eat avocados with organic ryvita. At least 1/3 avocado on organic rye toast will already do you a lot of good because it's flavorful and rich in fiber.

- **A powerful but light smoothie.** A mix of banana, blueberries, and some honey can be a powerful smoothie snack, especially after you've drank a mix of raw nut butter, greens, protein powder, and a fruit of your choice. A smoothie can perk you up and make you feel energized no matter what time of the day it is. Almond milk and frozen mixed berries will do the trick.

- **Dried fruit and whole nut bars.** It's your healthy kind of granola or trail mix and it's helpful because it's one of those things that you'd really love to snack on.

- **Bananas.** Bananas are full of the right amount of carbohydrates, sugar, fiber, and potassium so they are the best pre-workout and pre-game snack. Make sure to bring some with you at all times.

- **Baby Carrots/Carrot Sticks.** Baby carrots or carrot sticks might be a bit sweet, but they don't contain a lot of sugar and actually have loads of fiber that can sustain you and keep you on the go. Eat them with hummus or natural nut butter and you're all set!

Chapter 6: Preparing a few days before the event

The big day has arrived. You are about to put your hard work to the test. At this point you will know how competitive you will be, knowing your strengths and weaknesses. It is important at this point to be completely injury free. However, if you have a pinch here and a pull there, fret not! Once you are on stage, your adrenaline will be pumping and all your focus will be on the obstacle ahead.

Stay calm and concentrated. Bring your heart rate down by exhaling long breaths. You are ready! Once you push the buzzer and the people cheer you on, you'll be able to celebrate. Show your emotions and give the audience a show they won't forget. People will remember personalities even if they didn't make it to the final round. Kacy Catanzaro is still well know and will greatly benefit from her publicity, endorsing products or being accepted and competing the next year in American Ninja Warrior.

Here is a review of the main elements that you should now be able to master by the time you enter the stage.

Arm Movements or Brachiating

> You have to be comfortable hanging on rings and bars with one arm. Be able to hang for at least 30 seconds, without feeling too tired afterwards. Aim to be able to do a few one-arm pull-ups.

Prepping your grip

> Your grip has to be as strong as possible. Make sure that you don't only use rock climbing holds, but switch it up by using grips, such as ropes, cloth curtains, PVC pipes, pull-up bars, rings, and ledges so you can acquaint yourself with different materials and be prepared for what you have to face.

Upper Body Strength Training

You'll have superior upper body strength and coordination.

Adding Dynos to you climbing work outs can be extremely helpful when it comes to preparing for the American Ninja course. Dynos will teach you to hang on to the hold after a sudden jump. Take note that dynos require your full concentration. Be smart and don't get hurt! You have to train yourself not to be distracted and use whatever body part available to hang on.

Campus board training and leg-free climbing are extremely helpful. After a year of campus training you should be very comfortable going up and down the campus board several times in a row, doing double clutches.

While climbing by itself will strengthen your core, I would suggest to separately keep working on your abs at least four times a week using the above exercises.

Balance

Balance is key! As there are a lot of obstacles on the course, you need to make sure that you don't fall. Upper body strength and grip strength will do most of that job. However, obstacles like the Half Pipe Attack need your extreme focus and balance.

Parkour training will teach you all the balance that is required. However, if you don't choose to practice Parkour, train on balance beams, on rails, and eventually on a slack line. You can also practice on skateboards and balance boards.

Bouldering

As mentioned above, bouldering will be your new sport of choice, if you are serious about winning American Ninja Warrior. Climbing on vertical walls, overhanging walls, climbing dyno problems and traversing will all benefit you.

Aim to climb at least Level V5 in the gym and outside on natural boulders. Try wearing 10lb ankle weights in a fanny pack or make use of a weight vest as you move.

Footwork

Great footwork will help you with most obstacles. Again practicing Parkour or running through the forest or off the trails will prepare you to react to and overcome each new obstacle in your way.

Obstacle Challenges

Whether you are building and training on real size and spec American Ninja obstacles or whether you are building improvised versions as recommended above, you should be comfortable with the most challenging obstacles. Remember, you only have one try. So be prepared on what you will encounter on the American Ninja Warrior course.

Conclusion

Thank you again for purchasing this book.

The challenge now lies with you as you start preparing for the next season of American Ninja Warrior. Thousands of people prepare for this annual even. However, only a few will eventually make it to the finals in Las Vegas. What separates these few people from the rest of the competitors is their determination and work-out ethics. It is not enough to be physically strong, as one year of grueling workouts requires mental fortitude and strict discipline in diet and life style.

I know, if you follow this guide consequently and incorporate the work-out and diet suggestions in your training plan, you will without a doubt be fully prepared to compete on the show.

Lastly, if you enjoyed reading this book, if you have experienced improvements in strength and conditioning, or even better, if you made it to American ninja Warriors, I would love to hear from you. You can review this book on Amazon.com. Word-of-mouth is the independent author's best tool to be rewarded. And don't forget to mention this book, after you hit the final buzzer on Mount Midoriyama.

Good luck!

Appendix

Preview Of 'GMO Free Diet: The Ultimate Guide on Avoiding GMO Foods and keeping Your Family Healthy with a GMO Free Diet'

Busting the GMO Myths

Myth #01: GMOs increase the yield potential of the crop

Truth #01: GMOs DO NOT increase yield potential, they may even decrease yield potential of the crop.

High yield is regarded as a complex genetic potential that is based on multi-faceted genetic function. Therefore, increased yield can never be genetically engineered in any crop. Data obtained by earthopensource.org show that the non-GMO agricultural productivity in Western Europe is much better than the GMO productivity in the US. Agroecological practices and conventional breeding are still considered two of the top reasons for productive agricultural yields.

The US Department of Agricultural has released a report that contradicts this particular myth. According to a USDA report of 2002, 'commercially available, genetically modified crops do not show increase yield potential.' Another report in 2014 stated GE (genetically engineered) has not shown any augmentation in yield potentials. Moreover, the herbicide-tolerant seeds may offer lower yields if they contain BT or HT genes."

Myth #02: GMOs are climate change-ready.

Truth #02: Climate change resistance does not solely depend on plant genetics

GMO producers have claimed again and again that crops, which are genetically modified can withstand any severe weather conditions. However, this is completely false as weather resistance of crops highly depends on the complex and invariable genetic traits. Moreover, conventional breeding of crops is still way far ahead than genetic engineering when it comes to delivering crops that are truly climate-ready. Tolerance to climate change partly lies in agroecological techniques widely used today. Some commonly used techniques to prepare crops in extreme weather situations include diversity crop planting and soil building.

Myth #03: GMOs can help farmers reduce the use of pesticides/herbicides

Truth #03: GMOs prompt the use of more pesticides/herbicides

GMO producers have claimed that the production of GMO crops decreases the use of pesticides. However, this is completely untrue. Herbicide-tolerant GMOs make use of a significant amount of glyphosate-based chemicals (e.g. Roundup), which technically is a herbicide. In other words, the reduced pesticide used is replaced by a massive use of herbicide. Consequently, the growing cultivation of herbicide-tolerant crops has led to the production of 'superweeds'. This so-called 'chemical treadmill' in farming has been proven unsustainable and questionable, particularly for farmers in the southern hemisphere.

Myth #04: GMOs improve the nutrition content of the crops compared to naturally bred produce

Truth #04: GMOs have manifested nutritional side-effects caused by genetic alteration

"Healthier and far more nutritional value in agricultural crops" is the promise of GMO producers. However, there are still no nutritionally enhanced, genetically modified products available in the market. Moreover, due to the miscalculated effects caused by genetic engineering, there are now studies proving that GMO products are far less nutritious than their naturally grown counterparts. 'Biofortified' crops, such as the GM Golden Rice, are still not readily available in the market due to the ongoing toxicological testing.

Myth #05: GMOs can help reduce the risks of food shortage

Truth #05: Food security can only be achieved through agroecological farming

The International Assessment of Agricultural Knowledge, Science and Technology for Development (IAASTD) report in 2008, which was highly supported by 58 countries, points out that GM crops are not the key to food security. Moreover, the report highlights that GMOs cannot be endorsed due to safety concerns, inconsistent yields, and restrictive seed patents. The report also expressed that food security can be achieved through the agroecological system of food production. This report was based on a four-year project sponsored by World Bank and carried out by 400 scientists from 80 different countries.

To purchase this book go to http://amzn.to/1DEKJVz

Other Book Recommendations:

You Are Your Own Gym: The Bible of Bodyweight Exercises by Mark Lauren

Juicing for Health: The Essential Guide To Healing Common Diseases with Proven Juicing Recipes and Staying Healthy For Life by Donna Cavanaugh

The Ayurveda Hair Loss Cure: Preventing Hair Loss and Reversing Healthy Hair Growth For Life Through Proven Ayurvedic Remedies by Lila Kunda

"The Auto Immune Solution: Learn how to Prevent and Overcome Inflammatory Diseases and Live a Pain-Free Life" by Anthony Weil

Cannabis Oil Cures: How to cure cancer for life, improve health immediately, lose weight within 30 days and look younger with Cannabis Oil by Michael Skinner

"Edible Wild Plants for Beginners: The Essential Edible Plants and Recipes to Get Started" by Athea Press

On My Own Two Feet: From Losing My Legs to Learning the Dance of Life by Amy Purdy

Living and Dealing with Crazy People: The Ultimate Guide On How To Make Your Life Crazy-Proof by Michael Skinner

Made in the USA
Middletown, DE
08 September 2015